"DISAPPEARING INTO MYSELF: A MEMOIR OF LOST AND FOUND"

SHRESTHA RAYCHAUDHURI

Book Title: *"Disappearing Into Myself: A Memoir of Lost and Found"*

?

CHAPTER ONE: The Ache I Carry
Dear Me,

Somewhere between emptying the dishwasher and answering one more work email, I noticed something had quietly gone missing. It wasn't joy exactly, or purpose — those were still intact, like reliable old furniture in a house I built carefully. It was something smaller. Quieter. Like light slipping under a door that suddenly... wasn't there anymore.

Not sadness. Not despair. Just a subtle dulling. Like the bright, sharp edges of life had softened into pastels I never meant to choose. I still laughed. I still loved. But everything felt muted — like someone had turned the volume down without asking. And I only noticed when I leaned in to listen and heard silence.

There's an ache I carry that doesn't have a single name. But if I were to name it, I'd call it *the ache for intensity*. For the uncontained kind of feeling that used to surge through me like wildfire. The emotional chaos, the rush of becoming undone, the madness of being seen and chosen and wanted. I miss that kind of hunger. I miss being swept up in feelings that were so big, they frightened me a little.

In my twenties, I loved like my heart didn't understand consequences. I fell hard and often — and each time, it felt like I was cracking open. There was a wildness to it, a kind of sweet delusion that I now almost envy. Everything mattered so much — the brush of a hand, a glance that lingered too long, the trembling hope of being loved back with equal intensity.

I remember crying over someone once — sobbing, really — and feeling ridiculous and powerful at the same time. Ridiculous for letting someone get to me. Powerful because I could still *feel* that much. That kind of grief felt sacred, somehow. It meant I was alive.

And now? Now, I barely flinch.

When I met my husband, there was no cinematic swell of music. No sparks flying or time standing still. But there was something better, I told myself — something steadier. He's gentle. Good. He meets me with care and calm and consistency. He doesn't disappear when things get hard. He doesn't make love feel like a guessing game.

And I chose that. I still do.
But some days, I wonder: Did I trade in the high for the guarantee? And if so, why does part of me grieve what I left behind?

It's not about wanting someone else. It's not about being ungrateful. It's about craving *aliveness* — that feeling of teetering on the edge of something you can't name, but desperately want to jump into.

I miss infatuation — the delicious not-knowing, the nervous thrill of *what if*. I miss staying up late for no reason other than the promise of someone's voice on the other end of a glowing screen. I miss the way the right song at the right time could gut me, how a text could make my entire day feel different.

And now? I wake up, check emails, drink coffee, attend meetings, plan dinner, fold laundry, ask about deadlines, ask about groceries. There is rhythm. There is routine. There is even joy. But the wild color? That's gone.

The other night, I couldn't sleep. I sat on the kitchen floor with a blanket wrapped around me, staring at the humming fridge, asking myself questions I didn't want to answer. I tried to summon a memory that would make me feel again — really feel — but even the most vivid ones seemed distant, like I was remembering a movie I once loved but no longer understood.

I started leafing through an old journal I hadn't touched in years. The handwriting was chaotic, the emotions even more so. There were entries where I was sobbing onto the pages, ink smudged from tears, obsessing over a love I thought would undo me forever.

And I envied her.
Not for the pain. But for the *capacity*.
She was alive in every corner of herself — unashamed of wanting too much, of hoping too loudly, of falling without a parachute.

Now, everything is safer. More contained.
More "healthy," maybe. But also... flatter.

I want to believe that emotional saturation isn't something we only get to experience in youth. That being responsible doesn't have to mean being numb. That loving one person deeply and choosing them daily doesn't mean closing the door on that fire.

But I don't know how to access it anymore.
I don't know how to feel deeply without unraveling.

Sometimes, I catch glimpses. A song that hits a nerve. A scent that yanks me back. A dream that lingers all morning. But they pass too quickly. Like emotional ghosts. I reach out and they're already gone.

I guess that's why I'm writing this.
Not to go back. I don't want to relive old heartbreaks or chase old versions of myself.

But I want to *feel* again. Not just survive. Not just perform stability like it's the end goal of life. I want to wake up with a sense of possibility again.

This book — this confession — is not a complaint.
It's a search.
For depth. For aliveness. For the parts of me I've hidden under "being okay."
For the version of myself that doesn't just function — but *feels*.

This is where I begin.
Not with clarity.
But with truth.
And maybe, for now, that's enough.

With love,
Me

CHAPTER TWO: The Guilt of Being Unhappy When Everything Looks Fine

Dear Me,

I don't know what's more confusing — the fact that I've been depressed and anxious for the last three years, or the fact that I have no obvious reason to be. I keep asking myself: *Why am I like this?* Why, when everything on paper looks good — great, even — do I feel like this strange emptiness keeps following me around like a shadow that just won't back off?

I'm on medication. I take it daily. I function. I laugh. I work. I show up. And yet, there is a constant undercurrent — a quiet but persistent heaviness that never really lifts. Some days, I wonder if it's just a faulty wire in my brain. A chemical glitch. Maybe it's genetic. Maybe it's just the way I'm wired.

But then the guilt hits.

How dare I feel this way?

I have a loving husband. A family that cares. Friends who show up. A house that feels like the exact dream I built brick by brick in my head. I can travel anywhere, eat anything, buy whatever catches my eye — handbags, dresses, perfumes, whatever. On weekends, I socialize. I have deep conversations. I go out. I live.

But it feels like I'm living on the surface of a deep ocean I don't know how to swim in.

And so I spiral.

I ask myself if I'm just ungrateful. Spoiled. Maybe I haven't suffered enough to *earn* the right to feel this way. My life doesn't have the kind of suffering you read about in memoirs or watch in trauma documentaries. But that doesn't make it easier. It makes it lonelier.

Because pain without a name is harder to explain.

People want a reason. "*What happened?*" they ask. And when I say "Nothing really," they look confused. That confusion turns into discomfort. That discomfort turns into silence. And that silence makes me hide it again.

So I started laughing about it. Joking about how I root for Thanos. About how I cheered for the world ending in movies like *Thunderbolts* or *Infinity War*. About how I sometimes fantasize about some divine AI or climate change just wiping out humanity altogether — so that there's no more pain, no more inequality, no more slaughterhouses, no more cruelty, no more life.

Because life hurts.

Because humans ruin things.

Because even with all the good in the world, we're the only species that seems to destroy what it claims to love.

And no, I don't hate people. Not individuals. But humanity? I don't know. Sometimes I look at us and feel this deep, old resentment. We exhaust the earth, hurt animals, lie to each other, consume endlessly, compare everything, commodify feelings, sell happiness in the form of products, and then wonder why we all feel empty.

And the emptiness isn't even dramatic anymore. It's just... normal. A slow ache. A dull pain. Like background music.

So then I wonder — *What if it's not depression that's the problem? What if it's life that's a bit off-kilter?* What if the path we were told to follow — study, succeed, marry, settle — was always missing a chapter? What happens when you've ticked off the checklist of life and realize... no one told you what comes *after*?

I've done all the "right" things. And now what?

Where is the fire?
Where is the purpose?
Where is the *why*?

I used to think getting older would mean becoming more whole. But I didn't expect it to also come with the mourning — not just of my youthful face or energy, but of my *self*. The reckless, chaotic, hyper-feeling self. The one who used to hope for more. Now I mostly just want *less*. Less stimulation. Less suffering. Less of this world.

I started wishing for it to all just *stop*. The chaos, the noise, the bad news, the hate, the war, the greed. I say it out loud sometimes: *"If only the world would just end, there'd be peace."* I say it as a joke. But I mean it.

And people get scared. They don't know what to say. I don't blame them. I wouldn't either.

But I want to understand it. I want to hold space for this version of me that is angry, lost, and quietly drowning — not to fix her, but to *see* her. And when I finally did, I realized something important:

This isn't just about depression.
It's about disconnection.

Disconnection from meaning. From wonder. From purpose. From feeling like you *matter*.

The Solution? It's Not a Pill. It's a Path.

Let me be honest — meds help. They take the edge off. They let me function. But they don't fill the void. And I'm slowly learning, nothing *outside* of me will.

Not the vacations. Not the handbags. Not even the people I love. They help — of course they help — but they can't be my entire reason to feel alive.

I need to build a different relationship with life.
Not just to *live*, but to *feel*.

Here's what I've started doing — and what I'm still
learning to do:

1. **Stop Comparing My Pain**

My suffering is valid. Full stop. It doesn't need to be
justified by external hardship. Mental pain is real, even
when life looks shiny.

2. **Create Meaning, Don't Wait for It**

Maybe there isn't a grand purpose waiting to be
revealed. Maybe I have to *create* it. Maybe meaning is
something I sculpt out of the mundane.

3. **Redefine Success**

What if the next phase of life isn't about achievement
— but about depth? About finding new firsts. New
questions. New inner landscapes.

4. **Reconnect With Awe**

I've started paying attention to the small, strange
beauties. A certain light on the wall. A song that makes
me ache. A poem that punches my chest. I let myself
feel those moments.

5. **Let the Dark Thoughts Be Teachers, Not Enemies**

When I root for destruction in movies, I'm not evil. I'm
tired. I'm disillusioned. But that fantasy reveals a deep
longing — for peace, for simplicity, for a world that
feels just. And maybe if I honor that desire, I can
redirect it into building something better, rather than

burning it all down in my mind.

6. **Talk Without Editing**

I've learned to share the ugly thoughts — here, with myself, without shame. Not every friend will get it. But I do. And I need to keep listening.

I don't have all the answers. But I'm learning to sit with the questions without rushing to escape them. To mourn the past *and* make space for something new. To realize that maybe, life isn't about finding happiness — but about making peace with being human.

Even when being human is the hardest thing in the world.

With tenderness,
Me

CHAPTER THREE: Remembering How to Feel Alive Again

Dear Me,

I used to think life was a staircase — you keep climbing until you reach the top. Study hard. Get into the right school. Land the right job. Fall in love. Get married. Buy a house. Travel. Build a life that looks good from the outside. Tick all the boxes, one by one.

I did all of that.
And then... I looked around and realized there were no more stairs.

Just a wide, flat plateau.
And silence.

No next big thing. No mountain to chase. Just days. Routine. Comfort. Privilege, yes. But also — a kind of quiet despair.

No one tells you how disorienting it is to get *everything you thought you wanted* — and still feel this hollow ache. Like you're walking around in a life that should feel full, but instead feels oddly weightless. Like you're a guest in your own body. A ghost in your own home.

It made me question everything.
Who am I when I'm not striving?
What do I do now that the checklist is complete?
Is this it?

The scary part? It *could be*. It *almost* was. I could've settled into a life that looked fine and felt numb. I could've coasted. A version of me would've chosen that — the version that didn't want to rock the boat or seem ungrateful.

But another version of me — the one I had almost forgotten — whispered something else: *This isn't the end. This is the beginning.*

Because maybe *aliveness* doesn't come from chasing more. Maybe it comes from remembering what matters — not to others, but to me.

Who Am I, Really?

For so long, my identity was built on *doing*. On achieving. On being the responsible one, the dependable one, the "high performer." My self-worth was tightly tangled with what I could *produce*.

But what happens when you stop producing?

When there are no more metrics to beat? When there's no applause? When you wake up and realize you don't *have* to prove anything anymore — but you also don't know what to *feel*?

That's where I found myself.

So I asked a terrifying question:
Who am I, without all the roles I play?

Not the consultant.
Not the wife.
Not the daughter.
Not the friend-who-always-shows-up.
Just... me.

The first answer that came? *I don't know.*

The second answer? *Maybe it's time to find out.*

Redefining Purpose: From Proving to Becoming

Purpose used to be tied to proving something — to others, to the world, to myself. But I've realized that kind of purpose is exhausting. It always needs more. It keeps moving the finish line.

Now, I'm learning to let purpose be something quieter. Not a goal, but a direction. Not something to chase, but something to grow *into*. And weirdly, that feels more alive than any "success" ever did.

Aliveness, I'm learning, looks a lot like curiosity.
Like learning something new just because it lights you up.
Like making art without needing to be good at it.
Like sitting in silence and letting the world move through you.
Like crying at a poem. Or laughing at your own ridiculous thoughts.
Like starting over — not from scratch, but from honesty.

What Brings Me Alive Now

I started paying attention to what makes me feel *awake* in my body. Not in a performative, Instagrammable way — but in a *this makes my cells buzz* kind of way.

It's usually small, unexpected things:

- Writing like this. With no agenda. Just truth.
- Watching the rain and not needing it to stop.
- Going on long walks without headphones.
- Reading something that makes me pause and *breathe differently*.
- Crying at music, like really letting it gut me.
- Doing something badly — cooking, painting, dancing

— and *not caring*.

That's what aliveness feels like to me. Messy. Unstructured. Unproductive. But *real*.

And the more I allow space for that version of myself, the more I recognize her. She's not new. She's the younger me — the one who felt everything deeply, who looked for meaning in clouds and stories and strangers' faces. The one I buried under ambition and expectations.

I'm not trying to *go back* to her. I'm trying to *make space* for her — in this older, more tired, more complex body. We're both real. We both belong.

The Slow Rebuild

This isn't a movie montage. There's no dramatic turning point. Just small shifts. Gentle reawakenings.

I've stopped waiting for the next milestone to give me direction. I've started choosing *aliveness* as a way of being. And that has changed everything.

- I no longer need to be exceptional. I just need to be *present*.
- I no longer need to have it all figured out. I just need to be *curious*.
- I no longer need to chase the life I imagined. I need to *build* the one that *feels true*.

And here's what I know for sure:

**Purpose isn't a job title. It's a feeling.
Identity isn't a role. It's a relationship — with myself.
Aliveness isn't out there. It's here. Waiting. Quietly.**

Maybe the point of this phase of life is to stop climbing
and start rooting.

Not to rise above the world, but to sink into it.
To be deeply, wildly, unapologetically *human* — even when
it hurts.
Even when it's slow. Even when it doesn't make sense.

Especially then.

With a quieter kind of hope,
Me

CHAPTER FOUR: When Faith Feels Like Longing

Dear Me,

In my search for peace — not just the spiritual kind, but
the kind that could rescue me from my own heaviness — I
went to the Ramakrishna Mission and received mantra
diksha. It felt sacred, holy, like maybe this was the missing
piece. I thought it might be a kind of medicine for my
mind, a balm for the lingering fog of sadness that I
couldn't otherwise name.

I truly believed that if I chanted this mantra, if I showed
my sincerity to God, something would shift. My pain
would ease. My soul would rise. My mind would quiet.

I did chant it. For a few days, I tried. I tried to feel God's presence in the room, in my breath, in the rhythm of the words.
But then… I stopped.
Not because I stopped believing — but because I didn't feel what I was supposed to feel.

There was no sudden lightness. No transcendence. No permanent peace.
Just the same restlessness.
The same questions.
The same ache.

And what no one tells you — what scriptures sometimes skip over — is this:
Even devotion can feel empty. Even sacred practices can feel hollow when your heart is carrying too much grief.

I still believe in God. Fiercely. Maybe more than ever. But belief alone hasn't answered my questions — especially the deepest one:
If God is real, why is the world so full of suffering?

Why would a benevolent, all-powerful force create a man-eats-man world, a dog-eats-dog world, a rat race fueled by greed and cruelty and comparison? Why would a loving force allow for children to go hungry, for animals to be slaughtered mindlessly, for people to be used and broken and abandoned?

I know we're told God gave us free will. That we shape the world with our choices. That God gave us a canvas and it's

up to us to make it a paradise or a prison.
But sometimes, that just feels like a loophole. A way to blame humans for everything gone wrong, while God remains conveniently unaccountable.

And here's the conflict: I believe. But I'm angry.
I feel devotion and doubt in the same breath.
Some days, I'm chanting; other days, I'm yelling in my head at a God I can't see, begging for answers.

Sometimes I think — if I had even a fraction of God's supposed power — I would make things right. I wouldn't allow such immense, continuous suffering. And that thought fills me with guilt. How can I believe in God and still accuse Him of negligence?

That's when I spiral.

I start thinking about everything wrong in the world. The wars. The poverty. The slaughterhouses. The abuse. The loneliness. The betrayals. The silence.
And then I start thinking — maybe it would just be better if it all ended.

I've said things in half-jokes like "Let AI take over" or "Maybe climate change should just end the world." But sometimes I mean it more than I admit. I feel like cheering for villains in movies like Thanos or The Sentry, because at least they want to end the pain — even if it's through destruction. Even if it's wrong.

But underneath all that darkness, there's something else. Something fragile and buried:

A longing to be healed. A longing for the world to be healed.

I want to believe that things can be better. I want to see it. I want to experience it. Not in an afterlife. Not in some abstract salvation. But here. In this lifetime.

That's where spirituality gets complicated. Because it's not just about blind faith. It's also about grief. Sometimes we turn to God not because we're full of devotion — but because we're full of pain, and don't know where else to take it.

And maybe that's okay. Maybe that's still sacred.

What helped me begin to make sense of this was slowly realizing: **spirituality isn't about escaping the human experience. It's about transforming how we hold it.**

I started asking myself:

- What if God *is* present — just not in the ways I expected?
- What if God works through kindness, and not control?
- What if I saw God not as a puppeteer, but as a companion in the struggle?

When I stopped expecting God to fix things *for* me, and instead started noticing how life subtly nudges me toward deeper awareness, the narrative began to shift.

I realized I couldn't keep outsourcing my peace to divine interventions, vacations, material comforts, or even mantras I wasn't emotionally ready to connect with. I had to meet myself where I was: hurting, skeptical, tender, hopeful.

That's when I started looking inward. Not in a "fix yourself" way, but more like "listen to yourself" way.

I began exploring inner child work. Trying to understand the scared, innocent part of me that once believed in fairy tales and justice and happy endings — and who now feels betrayed by life.

I asked:
What did I stop believing in, and why?
What does the child inside me still long for?
And can I be the adult that child needed back then?

And then slowly, I started allowing spirituality to become less about "rules" and more about "relationship." A relationship with something greater. A relationship with myself. A relationship with the world, even in all its mess.

I don't have all the answers. I still can't make peace with every horror happening around me. I still cry when I think about animals in pain or people being bombed in some forgotten country.
But I also cry when I see someone helping a stranger, or saving a bird, or planting a tree. And maybe that's God too.

Maybe God is not the absence of suffering.
Maybe God is the presence that helps us endure it, change it, carry each other through it.

Maybe God is in the grief that makes us sensitive.
In the despair that pushes us to seek.
In the rage that tells us this world *should* be better.
And in the moments of love and awe that make us whisper, "Thank you," even on the hardest days.

This chapter isn't about solving anything. It's not about spiritual success or enlightenment.

It's just a reminder:
Your questions are holy. Your doubt is sacred. Your longing is real.
And you're allowed to keep believing, even if your belief has cracks.
That's where the light gets in.

Love,
Me

CHAPTER FIVE: The Good Person Myth

Dear Me,

I don't know if I'm a good person.
I know I'm not a bad one — but good?
I can't say that with certainty anymore.

Because if I were a good person, wouldn't I be doing more than *feeling bad*?

Like the other day — that injured pigeon on the road.
I saw it. My heart clenched.
Part of me wanted to run to it, cradle it, take it home, nurse it back.
But I didn't. I sat in the car. Frozen.
Scared. Helpless. Telling myself, *"Just pray for it. That's something."*
But it didn't feel like something. It felt like nothing.
Like guilt in motion.

And then there was the blind man who asked for directions.
I said, "Sorry, I don't know." Politely.
And walked away.
Only to realize five steps later that I *could* have helped.
Google Maps was right there in my phone.
I could've taken one extra minute.
But I didn't.
And it sat on me for the rest of the day — a quiet, gnawing shame.

These aren't dramatic failings.
I didn't harm anyone.
But maybe that's the bar I've set — *"I'm not hurting people. That's enough."*
But it doesn't feel like enough.

Because sometimes, not acting *is* a kind of harm.
Not helping *is* a kind of cruelty.

Not choosing *is* a kind of choice.

My husband tells me all the time:
"If you feel so much, why don't you *do* something?"
Join an NGO. Feed the strays. Donate.
"It'll make you feel better."
And I believe him. I *know* he's right.
But somehow, I never get to it.

I say *"I will"* — and I mean it in the moment —
But then the day passes.
The energy leaves.
The will evaporates.
And the next day begins, just the same.

And then comes the accusation that hurts the most:
**"You care so much about the world, but you don't care
about people close to you."**

And that one cuts deep.
Because it's true.

I can't remember the last time someone confided in me.
Not because I don't care, but because I think people sense
it —
That I can't hold sadness anymore.
That I absorb it too fast, and it drowns me.

People don't come to me with their pain
Because they know I might spiral with it instead of
helping them out of it.
I've lost the ability to listen without sinking.

And that's not empathy. That's emotional paralysis.

I've been told I'm cold. Aloof. Mean.
I've heard jokes about my *"resting bitch face."*
That no one wants to approach me.
That I look like I'm always angry.

And maybe — *maybe* — that's not an accident.

I've worn this expression like armor.
I've cultivated this "cool, distant, untouchable" aura on
purpose.
Because somewhere, growing up, I watched characters like
Sasuke, or Yagami Light —
Those cold, mysterious ones who didn't need anyone.
And I thought *that* was power. *That* was cool.

So I copied them.
I made myself unreachable.
A little arrogant. A little detached.
And now?

Now I don't know if it was ever an act — or if this is just
me now.

That's the terrifying part.
What if I've lost the softness for good?
What if the performance became the personality?

I want to believe there's still some tenderness left in me.
That the girl who wanted to help the bird, help the man,
help the world — still exists.

Buried, maybe.
Behind the cynicism. Behind the tiredness.
But still breathing.

Maybe this isn't about being a good person or a bad
person.
Maybe it's about being a **disconnected person**.

Disconnected from the softness I once had.
Disconnected from action.
From others.
From even myself.

And maybe it's not too late to re-connect.

Maybe being a "good person" isn't a fixed identity.
Maybe it's a muscle — one I haven't exercised in a while.
And like any muscle, it weakens with neglect. But it
doesn't disappear.

I'm not proud of the times I didn't help.
But I don't want to turn those moments into self-hate
either.

Because shame doesn't build kindness.
Only compassion does — even compassion for myself.

So I'm not going to label myself good or bad anymore.
I'm just going to try.

Try to pause.
Try to act.

Try to soften.
Try to help — in small, real, quiet ways.
Not to feel righteous.
Not to be seen.
Just to be *true* to that little tug in my heart that says, *"You could do something."*

That tug?
That's who I want to become again.

Love,
Me

CHAPTER SIX: The Quiet Room in a Loud House

Dear Me,

Last weekend, I said yes to something I usually avoid — a group game night.
"Truth and Dare."
A light, silly, social evening. Laughter, dares, childish games.
And from the moment I entered the room, I was drowning.

I looked around at the people — my age, my peers, my supposed community —
And all I could feel was: *alienation.*
Not disdain. Not superiority. Just this aching, unshakable **distance**.

The dares were playful. The energy was warm.
But inside me was this quiet, tired voice whispering:
"Why does this feel so performative? So… hollow?"

They laughed loudly. I smiled politely.
They joked and jumped and dared each other to act silly.
And I sat there thinking — *we're all in our 30s, why does
this feel like kindergarten with better cocktails?*
And then I felt guilty for thinking that.
Like I was the broken one — unable to access the joy
everyone else could.

It's not just the games. It's everywhere.
With friends at dinner, when they discuss office politics,
celebrity gossip, wedding outfits, vacation plans.
I listen, nod, sip my drink.
And internally, I feel myself slipping into that same cold,
blue water.
*"None of this matters. Why are we talking about this when the
world is burning?"*

But here's the truth:
I'm not proud of this alienation. I'm not proud of sitting in
judgment.

Because sometimes, I envy them.

I envy their ease.
Their laughter.
Their ability to immerse in the trivial without being
haunted by the existential.
I envy that they can talk about who wore what, or which

Netflix show to binge, without spiraling into questions about mortality, futility, or whether humanity even has a future.

My husband often reminds me — gently, and sometimes exasperatedly —
That not everyone *can* or *wants to* dwell in the depths all the time.
That what I call "trivial" might be someone else's sanctuary.
That these conversations, these cultural rituals, these everyday exchanges —
Are how people **survive** their own noise, their own chaos, their own fear.

And he's right.
I know he is.
But it doesn't change the fact that I feel *out of sync* with the world.
Not better. Not worse. Just... **out of rhythm**.

I've tried to "fix" this.
I've pushed myself to watch the shows, join the gossip, share memes, scroll through trends.
But it feels like wearing a coat that doesn't fit.
Every laugh feels delayed. Every opinion feels borrowed.
Every time I try to immerse myself in "normal," I end up feeling more fraudulent.

And what's worse is — this has started to isolate me.
I feel like I'm slowly disappearing from my friendships.
Not because I don't love them, but because I don't know

how to show up anymore.
I don't know how to be interested in what they care about.
And that makes me feel like a bad person.

Because I don't *want* to be aloof.
I don't *want* to be cold or distant or judgmental.

But I've built this wall — slowly, unintentionally —
A wall of apathy, boredom, withdrawal — and even a little
superiority.
A wall that looks like protection but feels like prison.

And here's where it gets darker —
Sometimes I wonder if I've lost the ability to **feel joy** in
simple things.
If I've become so addicted to intensity — to the heaviness
of philosophy and pain and purpose —
That I no longer know how to simply exist in the ordinary.

I find myself saying things like,
"What's the point?"
To shows.
To books.
To plans.
To people.

I start things and abandon them.
A movie, 15 minutes in.
A book, by chapter two.
A call, mid-ring.
A plan, mid-text.

It's not laziness. It's not distraction.
It's a kind of existential fatigue.
A numbness that makes everything feel like background noise.
A dull ache that whispers:
"This doesn't matter. None of this matters."

And yet — I *want* it to matter.
I want to care.
I want to *feel included*, not just present.
I want to laugh sincerely.
I want to belong in rooms again.

But I don't know how.
I don't know if I need to change myself, or just accept myself.
Whether this detachment is a phase, or the new reality.
Whether I'm protecting myself or isolating myself.
Whether I'm deep or just dissociated.

All I know is — I feel alone.
Even in rooms full of people who love me.

And I miss myself.
The version of me who could enjoy things without dissecting them.
The version of me who could sit in a group and *feel part of something* instead of floating above it, analyzing it, mourning it.

Maybe I'll find her again.
Or maybe I'll build a new version —

Someone who can live with the heaviness, but also learn
to dance in lightness.
Someone who doesn't have to choose between depth and
joy.
Someone who can hold both.

But today, I'm just trying to be honest.

Love,
Me

CHAPTER SEVEN: I Don't Know What to Call This Yet

I don't really know where this chapter begins. I don't even know if it *is* a chapter. Maybe it's just a moment. A quiet, restless kind of moment. The kind where the light in the room feels weird and your chest feels full but also sort of... empty? And nothing is *wrong*, exactly, but I want to crawl out of my own skin.

And I keep thinking — okay, *what is this?* What is this weird in-between feeling that follows me around lately like a shadow?

Is it boredom? Is it discontent? Is it just what being an adult feels like forever?

I don't know. And honestly, I'm tired of trying to name it.

What I *do* know is that I feel like I've drifted away from myself. Like... I blinked and suddenly I'm this overly responsible, overly tired person who *knows things*, who gets things *done*, but can't remember the last time she felt lit up from the inside. Like, really lit up. Spark-y. Hungry.

I used to *want* things. Not just checkboxes and tasks and career milestones. I mean real things. I used to want to dance in the kitchen with someone. I used to stay up late talking about nothing and everything. I used to write without wondering if it was good. I used to notice the way the air felt different before it rained.

Now I make lists. I manage calendars. I answer emails and fold towels and try to convince myself that stability is the same thing as aliveness. (It's not. It's really not.)

But I've been asking myself — did I choose this, or did I just stop choosing *anything else*?

Because somewhere along the way, I got really good at doing the things I'm supposed to do. Being thoughtful. Being organized. Being dependable. But the cost? I think it was me. I think I left parts of myself behind, slowly, without realizing. And now I don't know how to get back to her.

And here's the really honest part: sometimes I'm scared that if I slow down and stop performing "okay-ness," I'll realize how far I've actually drifted. How numb I've become. And what if I can't fix it?

But maybe it's not about fixing. Maybe it's just about *noticing*. Just *staying here*, with the weird ache and the fog and the longing and all of it — until something starts to make sense.

I keep hoping that if I sit in this long enough, it'll start to shift. Or soften. Or at the very least, stop feeling so lonely.

So yeah, I don't have a resolution here. No wisdom to offer. No steps to take. Just this:

I miss me. And I want her back. Not the reckless, dramatic version maybe — but the one who *felt things deeply* and didn't apologize for it. The one who could cry because a song hit too hard or because she felt *seen* in a movie. The one who still believed that something beautiful might be around the corner.

I want her. And maybe this is how I start looking.

Messy, confused, still a little detached, but... looking.

That has to count for something.

— Me

CHAPTER EIGHT: Okay, Maybe There's Still a Spark

This might sound stupid but I think I felt something today.

It wasn't huge. It wasn't fireworks or crying in the shower or anything dramatic like that. It was just... a flicker. A little jolt somewhere under the surface. Like someone tapped a light switch and the bulb blinked, just for a second, like *"hey... still here."*

It happened when I was walking home — and I wasn't rushing for once, wasn't on the phone or mentally adding groceries to the list. I just... walked. There was this weird golden light on the buildings. The air was that kind of crisp that smells like the edge of autumn. And I noticed it. *Really noticed it.*

And my brain went quiet for a second.
Just: *wow, this is nice.*

And that's not a big thing, I know. But I think it *is*, kind of. Because for a while now, even "nice" has been hard to feel. Everything's been muted, like someone turned the saturation down on my life. But today, for a few seconds, it was back. Color. Texture. A little spark of *aliveness*.

And I almost didn't write this down because it felt too small. Like — who cares? You saw some pretty light, good for you. But maybe that's the point. Maybe the flickers *start small*. Maybe they show up in the tiny cracks before they take up space again.

Like, maybe this is how I come back to myself. Not in one big sweeping moment, but in these tiny flashes of *wait — I remember this feeling.*

And yeah, it still hurts a little. Because when you feel again, you *feel* again. That ache comes back too. The longing, the "where have I been all this time?" feeling. The grief of lost versions of myself. But also... this weird flutter of possibility? Like maybe I'm not as lost as I thought. Maybe I've just been quiet. And maybe quiet isn't the same as gone.

God, I sound like I'm romanticizing a walk, but honestly? Who cares. If I can find magic in a sunset again, then that's something. That's a crack in the wall. That's a way in.

So here I am, holding onto that flicker. Letting it be enough for today. Not asking it to grow or mean anything yet. Just letting it exist.

It's small. But it's real.

And maybe — *maybe* — that means I'm still in here somewhere, waiting for the light to come back.

— Me

CHAPTER NINE: What Do I Do With This Flicker?

Okay so, I felt something. Great. Gold star for me. But now what?

I don't know how to hold this... whatever-this-is. This flicker. This sudden craving for more life, more *feeling.* I keep reaching for it like it's a doorknob, but when I grab it, my hand goes right through. It's slippery. Fleeting. But it's *there.* I know it is.

And now I keep noticing things. Like I'll hear a song and it hits different. Not like a gut punch — more like a gentle *tap-tap*, like "Hey. Remember when this would make you cry on the floor in the dark? Yeah. You used to *feel.*"

Or I'll be washing dishes and suddenly I'm flooded with this weird warmth. No trigger. Just... *here I am, alive in this body.*

And then five minutes later I'll be zoning out mid-conversation, spiraling into this random sadness that I can't explain. Like my body's catching up to everything I've ignored.

I don't know if this is healing or unraveling.

I don't know if I'm supposed to *do* something with this flicker or just... sit with it. Let it grow. Let it burn something down, maybe. Or light something up.

I started doing small things. Tiny experiments in feeling more. Like — I bought myself a stupidly expensive candle that smells like fig and memories. I journaled without trying to make the sentences pretty. I put on red lipstick just to go to the grocery store. I looked at the cashier *in the eye* and smiled like I meant it. I've been taking long walks with no podcast, no phone calls. Just me and my brain and the scary quiet.

And some days? It's nice. Peaceful.
Other days it feels like my thoughts are screaming at me, and I want to crawl out of my skin.

It's like my emotions are all waking up from hibernation and stretching their limbs and I'm just sitting here like — *oh. You're still here? Cool cool cool.* Totally not panicking.

Part of me keeps asking: *What's the point of all this?*
Another part goes: *Isn't the point just... this? Being in it.*
Noticing. Being a person again.

I don't know. I really don't.

But I do know this: I'm done numbing. I don't want to coast anymore. I don't want to live in grayscale. Even if it means feeling too much again. Even if it's inconvenient. Even if I cry in public. (Which I already did once last week. Outside a bookstore. Don't ask.)

I want to let things move me.
Even if it's messy. Especially if it's messy.

Maybe this is what it looks like — not a rebirth, not some grand epiphany. Just... one flicker at a time. One awkward, emotional, kind-of-beautiful moment after another.

I don't have a plan.

I just have this feeling.

And right now, that's enough.

— Me

CHAPTER TEN: When It Gets Too Loud

Some days it's a flicker.
Other days, it's a full-body collapse.

I'll be walking across the street and suddenly think,
What if a car just didn't stop?
Not in a tragic, movie-scene way.
Just... quick. Quiet. Done.
And then I shake it off like dust, but the thought stays.
Lurking.

I don't want to die. That's what makes this so hard to
explain.
It's not about wanting death.
It's about wanting everything to stop for a while.
Just... quiet. Stillness. Escape.
Like, *pause me.*
Please.

Sometimes I imagine falling — off a balcony, down stairs.
Not violently, just... *enough.*
I think about the relief of it.
Of being forced to rest.
Of someone else saying, *you don't have to do anything now.*
Because I'm so tired of holding everything up.
Of pretending I'm fine.

There's this pressure in my chest that doesn't go away.
Like grief and rage and exhaustion had a baby and it lives
in my ribcage.
Breathing feels like work.
Living feels like an endless to-do list.
Even joy feels like effort.

And I've done things I'm not proud of.
Small injuries. Scratches. Burns.

Not to die. Just to *feel*. Or to stop feeling so much.
To find some fucking relief from the noise in my head.

I want to scream sometimes.
I want to say, *I'm not okay*, but it feels stupid.
Because I have a good life.
Because I'm supposed to be grateful.
Because people would be *shocked*.

But that's the thing — I've become an expert at
performing okay.
Smiling. Small-talking. Delivering.
All while sinking quietly inside myself.

The panic attacks come like waves now.
Tight chest. Shaky hands. Dry mouth.
Sometimes I feel like I'm choking on nothing.
Like the air has turned against me.
I scratch at my arms, try to focus on textures, on sounds.
I count things.
I breathe like they tell you to.
It doesn't always help.

I wish I had something profound to say here.
I don't.
I just want to be honest.
Because the pretending is worse than the pain.

I think of that line people say — "I'm just tired."
But it's not the kind of tired sleep fixes.
It's the kind that sits in your bones.
The kind that makes even brushing your teeth feel

monumental.

Some days I get through by telling myself I don't have to
get through forever — just until the next hour.
And then the next.
And the next.
That's how I survive.

This chapter isn't tidy.
It's not hopeful.
It's me, in the middle of the ache, saying:
I'm still here.
Even when I don't want to be.
Even when part of me fantasizes about disappearing.

That matters.

So if you've ever looked at traffic and thought, *just one step,*
Or imagined what would happen if you didn't wake up —
You're not alone.
I'm with you.

Still here.
Still breathing.
Even when it hurts.

— Me

Absolutely. Here's **Chapter Eleven: Not Enoughness**
rewritten with those layers you mentioned — *imposter
syndrome, perfectionism, never liking what you produce.* Still
messy, still yours.

CHAPTER ELEVEN: Not Enoughness

I don't know where it started —
this feeling that no matter what I do, it's never quite it.
Never enough. Never right. Never good enough to be proud
of.
I can't even enjoy the things I create.
I finish something and immediately want to destroy it or
fix it or pretend I never touched it in the first place.
Every sentence, every idea, every version of me feels a bit
off.

There's always a better way I *should* have done it.
And someone out there who probably could have done it
better.
Cleaner. Louder. More convincing. More... something.

Sometimes I write things that people say are beautiful.
And I nod. Smile.
But inside, I feel like a fraud.
Like they're complimenting something that just got lucky.
Like they haven't seen *how much I hated it* five seconds
after I made it.
Like maybe I tricked them.

Imposter syndrome isn't even a shadow anymore — it's a
roommate.
It sits beside me at every table, in every meeting, reading
over my shoulder like,
"Hmm. That's what you're going with?"

There's this part of me that wants everything I do to be
perfect —
not because I think I'm brilliant — but because I'm scared
of what happens if it's not.
Like if I'm not perfect, then I'm nothing.
If it's not flawless, then it's not worth anything.
If I show something messy, I'll be exposed. Discarded.

I don't allow myself to get excited about what I make.
Because what if I love it and someone else doesn't?
What if I believe in it, and then it fails?
Better to downplay it. Undersell it.
Better to be the first to say "it's not that great," before
anyone else can.

There's always this tug-of-war:
Be excellent, but don't think too highly of yourself.
Achieve things, but don't make it look like you're trying too
hard.
Create, but hate it just enough to stay humble.

And the wild part is, from the outside, I think I look okay.
People tell me I'm capable. Talented. Kind.
But they don't hear the constant hum inside —
this loop of *"you don't belong here, you're not real, you're just*
faking your way through again."

I get paralyzed sometimes.
Not because I don't have ideas.
But because I don't think I'm allowed to own them.
Like who gave me the right?

Even when something good happens —
a win, a recognition, a breakthrough —
it doesn't land.
It bounces off. Like it was meant for someone else.
Like I must have slipped through the cracks and gotten
credit I didn't earn.

And it's so lonely, this space.
Because if I say it out loud, I sound ungrateful. Or
dramatic.
So I keep smiling. Keep producing. Keep doubting.

And no one sees how hard I'm working
just to believe that I might be... *okay.*
Not exceptional. Not perfect. Just okay.

I don't need to be the best.
But I'd like, just once, to feel *enough.*
Enough to exhale. Enough to say, "Yeah, I made that. And I
don't hate it."

That would feel like freedom.

-Me

CHAPTER TWELVE: The Mirror Lies but I Still Believe It

I can't remember a time when I didn't hate my body.
Even as a little girl, I was already pulling at my stomach in
front of the mirror, standing sideways, sucking in, hoping
the curve would disappear.
The heaviness, the softness — it felt like shame before I

even understood the word.
Like I was born into this skin, and the skin was wrong.

It's never been about being thin.
It's about feeling *worthy.*
About believing I have to punish myself for any moment
of happiness — like joy has a price, and that price is losing
weight.
If I don't lose enough, I don't deserve to smile.
I don't deserve to be proud of myself.
I don't deserve to be seen.

There's this number in my head — a weight.
A line drawn in sand that moves and shifts and never feels
quite real.
If I cross it, even a little, the walls close in.
Suddenly the clothes don't fit right, my reflection feels like
a stranger, and I spiral.
I cancel plans. I disappear.
I turn into someone I barely recognize.

And I've tried everything.
Starving until I'm dizzy, then binging until I feel sick.
Throwing up in the dark, wiping away tears in the
bathroom.
Excessive workouts that leave me trembling.
Drinking black coffee instead of eating.
All of it — a desperate attempt to feel *control* when
everything else feels out of reach.

Bulimia isn't vanity.
It's a war between hunger and shame.

It's shame wrapped in loneliness wrapped in an ache I
don't have words for.
It's crying alone, hiding empty wrappers, deleting and
reinstalling calorie apps like a vicious cycle I can't break.

Even on good days — when my clothes fit, when the
mirror shows a version of me that looks okay —
I don't believe it.
Compliments feel like echoes I'm not sure I deserve.
I don't trust myself to hold onto that image because the
voice in my head is louder —
"You'd be prettier if you lost five more kilos."
"You'd be lovable then."
"You'd finally be enough."

I weigh my worth in grams.
And every gram is a judgment.
A reminder of failure.

Sometimes I watch people eat without guilt, and I want to
scream.
I want their freedom.
I want to sit down to a meal and not spend the entire time
calculating, bargaining, planning how to undo it.
I want to enjoy dessert without the heavy cost of self-hate
afterward.
I want to wake up without the first thought being about
food or my reflection or the number on the scale.

But here I am, stuck in this endless battle.
Trying to love a body that feels like a cage.
Trying to find peace when my mind is a constant storm of

"not enough."
Not small enough. Not good enough. Not worthy enough.

I want to be able to look at a photo of myself and not zoom
in on the parts I hate most.
I want to stand in front of the mirror and find something
kind, something true.
But the truth is, the mirror lies.
And I keep believing it anyway.

I wish someone told me it was okay to be this messy.
That recovery isn't a straight line or a clean story.
That it's okay to stumble, to hate myself one day and try
again the next.
That self-love isn't about a perfect body or a perfect
number — it's about showing up, broken and scared, and
still choosing kindness.

People say, "Just love yourself."
But it's not that simple.
I wake up every morning trying to silence that voice that
tells me I'm not enough.
Trying to tell myself that beauty isn't a size, that worth
isn't a weight.
But the voice is relentless.

I'm tired.
So tired of fighting.
Tired of counting calories, weighing myself, punishing my
body for craving something as basic as food.
Tired of the endless loop where every bite is a battle and
every meal a test.

I want freedom.
I want to eat without guilt.
I want to move without shame.
I want to exist in this body without feeling like I'm
constantly failing it.

And maybe someday I will.
Maybe someday I'll find a way to silence the noise.
Maybe I'll learn to believe that my body is home — not the
enemy.
Maybe I'll be able to take up space without shrinking
myself.

But I'm not there yet.
Maybe that's okay.
Maybe the first step is just admitting the mess.
The pain.
The longing for something better.

So here I am, raw and real.
Not healed, not whole — but trying.
Trying to untangle the knots of shame and fear.
Trying to believe that maybe, just maybe, I can be enough
as I am.

And for now, that's enough.

-Me

CHAPTER THIRTEEN: The Weight I Carry in Their Eyes

It's hard to explain this feeling — the heavy, sinking sense that I'm a drain. That I'm sucking the energy and joy right out of the people who love me most. My partner, my family — the ones who should feel safe with me — sometimes I think they just feel tired. Not just tired, but *worn out* from me. Like I'm this weight they have to carry, and it's pulling them down day after day.

I watch them—my husband especially. When I'm spiraling, when the darkness curls around me tight and the panic rises, he tries to catch me, holds me steady. But I see it — the way his jaw clenches, the tightness around his eyes. He's trying not to show it, but he's tired. More tired than he lets on. I feel the exhaustion in his voice when he says, "I'm here," over and over, like a mantra, as if saying it enough will keep me from breaking apart completely.

And I feel guilty. Like a broken record repeating the same pain, the same fears, the same sadness. I know I'm not easy to love right now. I know it takes everything out of him and everyone else when they have to constantly be the ones comforting me. My family calls to check in, and I can almost hear the worry in their voice, the hesitation, like they want to ask if I'm okay but don't want to hear the answer. Sometimes I don't blame them for pulling back a little. Because how do you keep loving someone when all they do is hurt?

I feel like a liability. Not just emotionally, but in every way. Like I'm a burden that everyone around me is forced to carry. And if I disappeared — not in a dramatic way, but just *vanished* — maybe they'd finally be free. Free to laugh without worrying if I'm okay, free to make plans without canceling last minute because I'm stuck in a panic attack, free to live without the constant cloud of my sadness hanging over them.

And that thought, that wish, terrifies me. Because I want to live. I want to be here. But the part of me that's drowning thinks maybe they'd be better off without me. That my existence is this weight holding them back, stopping them from being fully happy. I wonder if they think about it too — if, in their most private moments, they imagine what life would be like if I wasn't the storm they have to weather.

It's a terrible, lonely place to be — to feel like you're both loved and resented at the same time. To know that you matter to people, but also know that your presence is a strain. That your pain, your silence, your breakdowns are this constant drain. And the worst part is feeling powerless to change it, to lighten the load.

But underneath all that guilt and fear, beneath the exhaustion and despair, there's this desperate longing. I long for them. Not just for their comfort, but for their joy. I want to be the one who brings light into their lives, who makes their days better — not harder. I want to be a source of peace, laughter, and love, not sadness and worry.

I imagine what that would be like. To have a conversation where I'm not the one falling apart. To make someone smile because of me, not in spite of me. To be someone they look forward to seeing, someone who gives energy back instead of draining it. I want to give them the gift of me at my best, not the weight of me at my worst.

But right now, that feels like a distant dream — like something I'm not sure I deserve. Because when I look at myself, I see someone fragile, broken, tangled up in thoughts and feelings that feel too big to carry. Someone who needs help more than she can give it. Someone whose presence sometimes feels like a problem instead of a blessing.

I'm terrified that the more they have to carry me, the more they'll grow tired and resentful. That my partner, my family, will start to see me not as the person they love, but as the person they *have* to love. And maybe, deep down, I'm scared they already do.

And yet — despite all of this — I'm still here. Still holding on. Still loving fiercely even when it hurts. Still wanting to be better, to be lighter, to be someone who adds joy instead of taking it away.

Maybe that's what love is — carrying each other's burdens, even when it feels impossible. Maybe it's about staying even when you want to run away. Maybe it's about finding small moments of light in the darkest storms.

So I keep trying. Even when I feel like I'm drowning in this weight, even when I want to disappear, I keep trying to be present. To be patient with myself. To hold space for both my pain and my hope.

Because maybe someday — someday soon — I'll stop feeling like a liability. Maybe someday, I'll find a way to give without breaking. Maybe someday, I'll believe I'm enough.

But until then, I carry this ache — this messy, complicated ache — and I hold onto love.

And that has to be enough.

-Me

CHAPTER FOURTEEN: The Beginner's Loop

I start things. I really do. With so much fire and excitement that sometimes I wonder if the thing I'm about to dive into will become the next big part of me. The next identity, the next passion. But somehow, it never sticks. I never make it past the beginning.

There was the violin — that beautiful, impossible instrument that sang with the kind of magic I wanted inside me. I remember the first few lessons, gripping the bow awkwardly, feeling like I was holding a secret language. And then, after a while, the notes got harder. The finger placements confusing. The practice felt like a chore, and slowly I stopped picking it up. It sat in its case, silent, waiting for me to come back. But I never did.

Bharatanatyam was even more intense. The rhythms, the mudras, the storytelling through movement — it was like learning a language that lived inside your body. I loved

how it made me feel connected to something ancient and
sacred. But then the schedules, the tiring rehearsals, the
self-consciousness — it all piled up. And just like that, I
stopped showing up. The music played on without me.

Painting was supposed to be my escape. Colors splashing
freely, brushstrokes that could say what words couldn't.
I'd sit with a canvas, bright-eyed, imagining masterpieces.
But every time I looked at what I'd made, I felt like it
wasn't good enough. So the brushes dried out, and the
canvases piled up blank.

Reading is the one I come back to the most. But even there,
I never finish. I pick up a book with a thrill, start turning
pages fast, then get distracted — by my phone, by my
thoughts, by the endless "to-dos." Half-read books clutter
my shelves, little monuments to my impatience.

Embroidery, writing this book, cooking, candle making,
soap making — they all start the same way: a rush of
inspiration, a weekend of obsession, and then silence. I'm
excited, I'm passionate, I want to learn and create and *be*
good at it. But soon enough, the momentum slows. The
hard parts start. The learning curve steepens. And I bail.

There's this ache in being the eternal beginner — always
at the start line, never crossing the finish. Always chasing
mastery but never quite catching it. It's frustrating. It feels
like a mirror to other parts of my life — the perfectionism,
the self-doubt, the fear of failing.

And maybe that's the truth. Maybe I'm scared of what happens when I'm no longer a beginner. When I'm good. When I have to own the time, the effort, the commitment. Because what if I fail then? What if the thing I love isn't enough to carry me forward?

But maybe the answer isn't in finishing or becoming proficient. Maybe it's in loving the messy, clumsy process of starting. In letting myself be curious, even if I don't stick around. In learning to be okay with being a beginner forever.

Because every time I pick up the violin, or the brush, or the needle — I'm showing up for myself. I'm telling myself I'm worth the effort, even if just for a little while. And maybe that's enough.

Maybe being a beginner is my way of holding onto hope — hope that someday, maybe, I'll find the thing that won't let me go. Or maybe I'll find peace in starting without needing to finish.

Either way, I'm here. I'm trying. And for now, that's enough.

CHAPTER FIFTEEN: The Quiet Turning

It's hard to explain how change happens inside you — how sometimes the darkest, most tangled parts of yourself start to soften, how a tiny spark flickers in the places you thought were long dead. I don't think this is some big epiphany moment. I don't think it's a clear line between 'before' and 'after.' It's messy and slow and full of second-guessing and falling backwards almost as much as it's full of moving forward. But I can feel it. Something is different now. I don't know if I'd call it peace exactly, or happiness, but maybe something in between — a kind of fragile, quiet turning.

For years, I've been caught in a storm of my own making — beating myself up for every little misstep, drowning in the weight of my own thoughts, dragging myself through the dark nights of the soul where nothing feels right and every breath is heavy. I carried around this feeling of never being enough — not good enough, not strong enough, not capable enough — like a secret shadow that never quite leaves my side. I was always chasing something — perfection, approval, meaning — and somehow the harder I chased, the further it slipped away.

And in that chase, I lost myself a little bit each time. I lost the joy I used to find in simple things, the spark of curiosity that made me want to try new things or write or paint or just be. I started to feel like a stranger to my own life, like I was watching myself from the outside, moving through the motions but not really living. I hated that feeling. I hated how disconnected I was — from my body, from my emotions, from the people I loved.

But now I'm learning — slowly, painfully — that feeling disconnected doesn't have to be permanent. That maybe the way back isn't about fixing or forcing or grinding harder. Maybe it's about slowing down. About being honest with myself, even when that honesty is ugly or scary. About letting myself feel the mess instead of trying to tidy it all up.

This book — these pages full of my fears, my failures, my confessions — they're part of that process. Writing it has been like peeling back the layers, exposing the parts I usually hide away. And in that exposure, I'm finding something unexpected: a kind of freedom. Freedom to be imperfect. Freedom to be vulnerable. Freedom to say, "I'm not okay" and still be worthy of love and kindness.

I think that's the biggest lesson I'm learning: I don't have to be fixed to be lovable. I don't have to be perfect, or productive, or always strong. I just have to be me — all of me, the light and the dark, the messy and the beautiful. That's hard to accept because it means I have to sit with my pain without running from it. It means I have to face the parts of myself I'm ashamed of, the parts I want to hide. But it also means I can start to heal.

And healing isn't a straight line. Some days, the weight feels unbearable again. The tightness in my chest, the panic creeping in, the urge to hurt myself, to escape — those things haven't gone away completely. But they feel a little less like the whole story now. There's space around them. There's room for hope, even in the dark.

I'm still scared, so scared, of being a burden to those I love. I hate that my pain sometimes drags them down or makes them worry. I hate feeling like I'm sucking the joy out of their lives. But I'm learning to ask for help anyway. To say when I'm struggling instead of shutting down or pushing people away. And when I do that, I'm reminded that love isn't about perfection or endless strength — it's about showing up, even when it's hard.

The people who stick around — my husband, my family, my friends — they remind me that I'm not alone. They remind me that I'm worth their time and their care, even on my worst days. Sometimes, I catch glimpses of that love, and it feels like a warm light in the cold. I'm starting to trust that maybe, just maybe, I don't have to carry everything on my own.

I'm still figuring out what "feeling more" really means. It's not always the intense, overwhelming emotion I imagined. Sometimes it's quiet — a soft smile, a deep breath, a moment of peace in the chaos. Sometimes it's taking care of myself when I want to push away or numb out. Sometimes it's letting myself cry, or rest, or just be.

And I'm beginning to realize that I don't have to be afraid of my feelings. Even the hard ones — sadness, anger, fear — they're part of me. They don't make me weak; they make me human. When I stop fighting them, when I let them come and go like waves, I feel less trapped. More alive.

I'm learning to celebrate the small wins. Like getting out of bed on a tough day. Like writing a page, even when the words don't feel perfect. Like playing the violin for five minutes, even if I'm terrible at it. Like cooking a meal that doesn't burn. These little moments add up. They remind

me that progress isn't about giant leaps; it's about steady
steps.

And those hobbies I've started and abandoned? I'm not
calling them failures anymore. They're part of my story
too. They show that I'm curious, that I'm willing to try,
that I'm alive. Maybe one day I'll find the patience to stick
with one of them. Or maybe I'll always be the beginner —
and that's okay. Being a beginner means there's always
room to learn, to grow, to surprise myself.

I want to hold on to this turning — this quiet shift inside
me. I want to keep moving forward, even when it's slow,
even when it's scary. I want to keep loving myself enough
to ask for help, to set boundaries, to rest when I need to. I
want to keep opening my heart, even if it means risking
pain.

Because I believe — really believe — that healing is
possible. That joy can come back. That peace can exist
alongside pain. That I can live a full, messy, beautiful life,
just as I am.

So here I am. Still imperfect, still afraid, still struggling.
But also hopeful. Also brave. Also ready.

Ready to keep turning, keep learning, keep loving.

Because this life — with all its mess and beauty — is
worth it.

And so am I.

Contents